A ROOKIE BIOGRAPHY

RACHEL CARSON

Friend of Nature

By Carol Greene

 CHILDRENS PRESS®

CHICAGO

This book is for Madeline Ericson.

Rachel Carson (1907-1964)

Library of Congress Cataloging-in-Publication Data

Greene, Carol.
    Rachel Carson : friend of nature / by Carol Greene.
      p. cm. — (A Rookie biography)
    Summary: A biography of the biologist whose writings helped initiate
the environmental movement.
    ISBN 0-516-04229-7
    1. Carson, Rachel, 1907-1964—Juvenile literature. 2. Biologists—United
States—Biography—Juvenile literature. 3. Environmentalists—United
States—Biography—Juvenile literature. [1. Carson, Rachel, 1907-1964.
2. Biologists. 3. Environmentalists. 4. Science writers.] I. Title. II. Series:
Greene, Carol. Rookie biography.
QH31.C33G74   1992
574'.092—dc20
[B]   91-39446
                                      CIP
                                       AC

Rachel Carson
was a real person.
She was born in 1907.
She died in 1964.
Rachel wrote important
books about nature.
This is her story.

TABLE OF CONTENTS

The Carsons' house in Pennsylvania (above) was surrounded by woods and fields. Young Rachel (right) picked flowers in the garden.

Chapter 1

Far From the Sea

Little Rachel Carson
lived in a house
with woods and fields
all around.
She spent long days
in the woods and fields.

Rachel's mother taught
her about plants and
trees, birds and insects,
and small, furry animals.
Rachel loved to
learn about nature.

Mrs. Carson with her children
Marian, Rachel, and Robert

But Rachel's home was in
Springdale, Pennsylvania,
far from the sea.
And Rachel wondered
about the sea.

Rachel also loved to
read and write stories.
She thought she might
be a writer someday.
So she read and
wrote a lot.

Rachel, shown at left
with her dog Candy.
The sea fascinated
young Rachel.

6

When Rachel was 10,
she sent one of her stories
to *St. Nicholas*,
a children's magazine.
They published it!
Maybe she really *could*
be a writer someday.

All through high school,
Rachel worked hard.
She won money to help
her go to college.

At Pennsylvania College
for Women, she worked hard, too.
Some of her stories
were published
in the college magazine.

"Rachel is a fine writer,"
said her teachers and friends.

But the college
was in Pittsburgh,
Pennsylvania, far
from the sea.
And Rachel still
wondered about
the sea.

Rachel with her
mother and father

One rainy night,
she sat in her room,
reading a poem.

"For the mighty wind arises,
roaring seaward, and I go."

All at once, Rachel's
heart felt full.
She knew for sure
that someday she
would go to the sea.

At the Pennsylvania College for Women (above), Rachel (below; top row, second from right) played on the Honorary Hockey Team.

Chapter 2

What Rachel Did

"Did you hear what
Rachel Carson did?"

Everyone at college
was talking about her.
Rachel Carson,
that fine writer,
had decided to study zoology,
the science of animals,
instead of English.

Rachel (right) and her college teacher, Mary Scott Skinker

It started with one
class and a very
good teacher named
Mary Scott Skinker.

She taught Rachel
about the lives and
ways of different
living things.

Rachel wanted to learn
more—and more.
She took six science classes
her last year in college,
and she graduated
at the top of her class.

Rachel Carson as a college senior

Rachel also won money
to study at a famous
university, Johns Hopkins.
Best of all, she could go to
a lab to study sea life at
Woods Hole, on Cape Cod
in Massachusetts.

Woods Hole, Massachusetts

At last Rachel Carson
was going to the sea.

Rachel spent six happy
weeks at Woods Hole.
She met scientists from
the United States government's
Bureau of Fisheries.

"Someday I want to work
there, too," decided Rachel.

But first she studied hard
at Johns Hopkins University.

Johns Hopkins University is in Baltimore, Maryland.

Then, in 1929, the
stock market crashed.
The Great Depression
began, and many people
lost their jobs.

Back in Pennsylvania,
Rachel's family had no work.
But Rachel was doing
part-time jobs
while she went to school.
So she rented a house
near Baltimore, Maryland,
and asked her parents
to come live with her.
They'd all be poor together.

Rachel was 22 when she was
accepted at Johns Hopkins.

At last, in 1932,
Rachel got her degree
in zoology from
Johns Hopkins.

But then Rachel couldn't find a full-time job.

So she taught part-time at Johns Hopkins and the University of Maryland.

In 1935, her father died. Now Rachel had to earn more money. She went to see Elmer Higgins at the Bureau of Fisheries.

Elmer Higgins was the chief of the biology division of the Bureau of Fisheries.

"Can you write?" he asked.
He needed a scientist
to write radio stories
about life in the sea.

Could Rachel Carson *write?*
She surely could.
At last she got a part-time job
at the Bureau of Fisheries.

Rachel studied sea life from
boats like the *Albatross* (above left).
Heavy, old-fashioned diving
helmets (right) were used for
deep-sea exploration.

Chapter 3

Books

One day, Rachel took
a government test.
She was the only
woman who took it,
and she got the top score.

Now she had a full-time
job with Mr. Higgins.

Before long, he asked her
to write something else
about the sea.

"Who has known the ocean?
Neither you nor I,"
began Rachel.
She wrote a beautiful piece.
But Mr. Higgins gave it back.

"Send this one to
the *Atlantic*," he said.
The Atlantic Monthly
was a magazine that
used beautiful writing.

Rachel sent her piece
and the *Atlantic* bought it.
When it came out, a man
from a publishing company
read it and wrote to Rachel.

"Have you thought about
writing a book?" he asked.

A book?
When could she write a book?
She worked all day.

Rachel Carson (right) studying sea life at the shoreline

Rachel's pet dog models her sunglasses in a
playful moment at the house in Silver Spring, Maryland.

And at home, in a house
in Silver Spring, Maryland,
she helped care for her nieces.
Their mother had died, so
the two little girls lived
with Rachel and her mother.

Rachel had no time.
But she wanted
to write that book.
So she made time.
She wrote late at night,
and her cats kept her company.

Under the Sea-Wind
came out in 1941.
It told about life
on the shore,
in the open sea,
and on the sea
bottom.

**A tidal pool
on the southern
coast of Maine**

Other scientists liked it.
But World War II had just
begun, and people were
not buying books.
So it didn't make much money.
Rachel sighed and went
on with her other work.

In 1948, she had an idea
for another book.
A friend helped her get
an award for writers.
Rachel needed the money
to take time off from her job.

Rachel Carson in 1951

The Sea Around Us
came out in 1951.
It told about life in
all the world's oceans.
It said how much
people need the oceans.
And it was a best-seller!

Now Rachel could afford
to quit her job and
write whenever she wanted.

The California coast (above). A palm
tree (below right) grows near the shore in Jamaica.
Coral (below left) is found in warm seas around
the world. All these environments are
influenced by the seas around them.

Chapter 4

Silent Spring

Years went by and
Rachel kept writing.
The Edge of the Sea
came out in 1955.

It told about life
along the Atlantic
coast . . . the rocky
shore, the rim of
sand, and the coral
coast. It even told
the life of a
grain of sand.

Rachel Carson studying
a tidal pool in Maine

Rachel and her adopted son, Roger

Rachel's nieces grew up.
In 1957, one niece died.
Rachel adopted her
little boy, Roger.

She was working on
another book in 1958.
Then she got a letter
from a friend, Mrs. Huckins.

Planes had sprayed DDT
in Mrs. Huckins' neighborhood.
DDT was a chemical
used to kill insects.
But Mrs. Huckins saw
that DDT killed
songbirds, too.

This advertisement was supposed to show that DDT was a safe pesticide. But Rachel Carson found that it was harmful to many living things.

Rachel Carson
watching hawks
flying above
Hawk Mountain
in Pennsylvania

Rachel knew that DDT
could kill many animals.
Someone had to write about
the dangers of such chemicals.
Before long, she knew
that she was the one.

"There would be no peace for me
if I kept silent," she said.

She learned many facts
about pesticides and how
they can harm the earth.
Then she began to write.

Rachel called her book
Silent Spring.
She said that one day
springtime *would* be silent
if pesticides killed the birds.

Two of Rachel Carson's
best-selling books

Rachel Carson worked
hard to become a
scientist. So
when Rachel told
the U.S. Senate
about the dangers of
pesticides (below),
they believed her.

Pesticide companies
tried to fight Rachel.
They said she didn't know
what she was talking about.

But Rachel was a scientist.
She knew the facts
about pesticides.
Her book has taught
people everywhere to take
better care of the Earth.

Chapter 5

A Sense of Wonder

Rachel felt very tired as
she worked on *Silent Spring*.
At last her doctor told her
that she had cancer.
She would not live long.

Rachel wanted to write
many more books.
One would be based on
a magazine article
she had written earlier.

Rachel wanted all
children to share
her sense of wonder
about the things
of nature.

The article was about
children and nature.
Rachel told of the good times
she and Roger had
in the woods and by the sea.

She wanted all
children to have
"a sense of wonder"
about the things
of nature:
giant waves and
tiny plants,
blazing stars and
chirping insects.

Rachel holding
a starfish

A memorial at the Rachel Carson National Wildlife Refuge in Wells, Maine

Rachel did not have time
to write that book.
She died on April 14, 1964.
She was only 56.

Other people put photos
with her article.
They made a book called
The Sense of Wonder.
It came out in 1965.
Rachel would have liked that.

The wildlife refuge below was named for Rachel Carson.
Above: Rachel (right) at a publisher's party in 1957.

Rachel Carson received many
awards for her writing.
They made her happy.

Because of Rachel Carson's work, many people now realize that we must protect our natural world.

But the things of nature
that she saw with
her own sense of wonder
made her even happier:

An orange butterfly,
a spring morning full
of singing birds,
and, of course, the sea.

45

Important Dates

1907   May 27—Born in Springdale, Pennsylvania, to Maria and Robert Carson

1917   Sold story to *St. Nicholas* magazine

1925   Went to Pennsylvania College for Women, Pittsburgh

1929   Went to Johns Hopkins University

1936   Began work at United States Bureau of Fisheries

1941   *Under the Sea-Wind* published

1951   *The Sea Around Us* published

1955   *The Edge of the Sea* published

1962   *Silent Spring* published

1964   April 14—Died in Silver Spring, Maryland

1965   *The Sense of Wonder* published

INDEX

Page numbers in boldface type indicate illustrations.

PHOTO CREDITS

ABOUT THE AUTHOR

Carol Greene has degrees in English literature and musicology. She has worked in international exchange programs, as an editor, and as a teacher of writing. She now lives in Webster Groves, Missouri, and writes full-time. She has published more than 100 books, including those in the Rookie Biographies series.